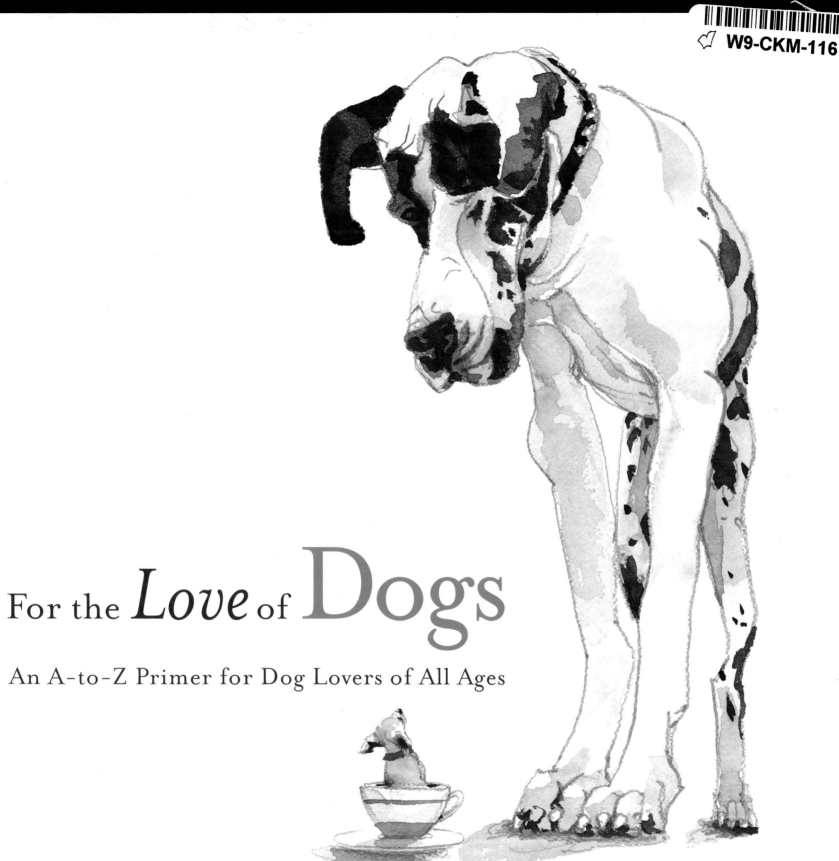

For the *Love* of Dogs

An A-to-Z Primer for Dog Lovers of All Ages

Written by **Allison Weiss Entrekin** Illustrated by **Mark Anderson**
Foreword by **Victoria Stilwell**

"P" is for many things...
poodles, paws, puppies.
But to me, "P" will always stand
for one word: *Positive*.

I'll explain.

When I was a little girl growing up in Wimbledon, England, I wasn't allowed to have a dog. Both my parents worked, and it was just too much for them to add another creature to our busy household. Still, my grandmother's life was her Beagles, and because I spent a lot of time with her during my youth, her love of dogs rubbed off on me.

I pursued acting as a young adult, and I walked dogs as a way to supplement my income. I found that I was quite good at it—within one month, I had more than 20 clients. I didn't understand it at the time, but dogs were drawn to my positive approach to relating to them. I didn't focus on dominance; I focused on cooperation.

From there, I embarked on a fascinating journey in which I sought to learn about dogs and the incredible bond we humans share with them. I volunteered at rescue shelters. I read every book I could get my hands on. I attended seminars. I educated myself as best I could. And finally, I made myself "official" and became certified in animal training and behavior.

Well, we all know what happened next—I continued to work with dogs, television producers found my approach interesting, and now I have my own series, *It's Me or the Dog*, and serve as a judge on *Greatest American Dog*. I still believe passionately that dogs respond best to positive reinforcement training methods rather than punitive, dominance-based techniques. So to me, "P" is for positive—always has been, always will be.

Of course, "B" is for books, and I certainly love this one. Its fantastic poems and clever illustrations have made it a hit in my house, where my husband, daughter, and Chocolate Lab, Sadie, all read it together. It reminds us of the deep, loving, and sometimes humorous bond we all share—and that's pretty darn positive, too.

–Victoria Stilwell
World-renowned dog trainer and host of It's Me or the Dog

For more information about Victoria, please visit her official site, www.positively.com.

"A" is for Adoption.

Though dogs like to roam,
Every last one knows
There's no place like home.

Every year, approximately 7 million dogs and cats enter shelters in the United States. They range from young to old, small to large, mixed-breed to purebred (in fact, the Humane Society of the United States estimates that as many as 25 percent of all shelter dogs are purebred). Each of these animals deserves to be adopted into a loving, forever home, but unfortunately, statistics show that only about half of them will exit shelters with a family. To find out more about animal adoption and how you can help, visit www.humanesociety.org.

"B" is for

Beagles,

A howling good breed.
They'll wake up the neighbors
But love you indeed.

Beagles' penchant for baying prompted the French to call them *be' gueules* ("gaping mouths"), which led to their current name, Beagles. They are happy hunting dogs whose most famous family member is Snoopy from the *Peanuts* comic strip. Like Snoopy, they are even-tempered and caring toward people. Their sweet disposition, coupled with their small size and low-maintenance coat, make them ideal pets for many people. Beagles have historically placed among the top-five most popular breeds in the United States, according to the American Kennel Club.

"C" is for Cavaliers,

The spaniel of kings.

They want (and receive)

All of life's finer things.

Cavalier King Charles Spaniels were named after **King Charles II of Britain** (who reigned during the 17th century), and countless paintings and tapestries depict their ancestors posing with aristocratic families. Known for their playfulness and good humor, Cavaliers generally get along with everyone from babies to large dogs. These pups aren't afraid to be pampered—they love having their long, silky ears brushed, and they're happy to curl up in their parents' laps for a snooze.

"D" is for
Dachshunds.

Their spunky demeanor
Makes them America's
Real favorite wiener.

Dachshunds may be short in height, but they're long on personality (their bodies are pretty long, too!). Always tenacious, they'll chase squirrels and bark at much larger dogs with reckless abandon. Perhaps that's why the Germans call them "badger dogs!" Because of their build, they are sometimes referred to as "wiener dogs" in the United States. There are three fur varieties among Dachshunds—smooth, wirehaired, and longhaired. The breed as a whole is traditionally one of the top-10 most popular in the country, according to the American Kennel Club.

"E" is for
English Foxhounds;

They're jolly good Brits.
They'll spend the day hunting
Then have tea and biscuits.

As their name indicates, English Foxhounds trace their roots to Great Britain, where they were bred to hunt foxes. Full of energy, they love to run...and run...and run. (Good apartment dwellers, they are not!) They like being with other dogs or people as part of a pack; this is how their ancestors traveled while on the hunt. They are the short, stocky, and slightly slower cousins of American Foxhounds and a favorite subject of painters who create hunting scenes.

"F" is for the

First Dog,

A puppy named Bo.
He has reached the highest office
A canine can know.

In 2009, the Obama family received a gift from Senator Ted Kennedy—a Portuguese Water Dog named Bo. This helped President Obama fulfill his campaign promise to his daughters that he would let them have a dog once the election was over. Bo is an upbeat and feisty fellow who keeps Sasha and Malia Obama company in the White House, and he's even allowed to roam inside the Oval Office with the president himself. Still, President Obama insists he will not allow the pooch to share a bed with him; at press time, he still hadn't caved.

"G" is for

Golden Retriever.

They'll turn your clothes blonde,
But teach you that love
Is a powerful bond.

Whether they're serving as guide dogs, search-and-rescue dogs, or simply family dogs, Golden Retrievers excel at what they do. Their long, golden coat is beautiful to behold, but it also sheds seasonally, which means their people are usually covered in hair. But these dogs are worth a few extra lint brushes—intelligent and eager to please, they are widely considered one of the most loving breeds. Golden Retrievers have historically ranked among the top-five most popular breeds in America, according to the American Kennel Club.

"H" is for

Hooch.

We'll never let go
Of the story of Turner
And his Dogue de Bordeaux.

Turner and Hooch, the 1989 comedy starring Tom Hanks, was a box-office success thanks in no small part to the lovable "Hooch," its Dogue de Bordeaux headliner. Like Hooch's character, Dogues are large, a bit slobbery, and very loving, true guardians with loyal hearts. They're affectionate with people, but they're not afraid to protect their homes if they feel threatened. Sometimes referred to as French Mastiffs, these dogs can weigh up to 110 pounds, and their heads are considered the largest in the canine world.

"I" is for Instincts,

The things dogs just do.

Like bark at a stranger—

Or chew up your shoe.

Dogs have a number of inborn tendencies that can **vary from breed to breed**. Some like to dig, while others prefer to chase. Some bark at strangers, while others hide in tight spaces. Depending on when these instincts occur and to what degree, they can be heroic, infuriating, or just plain funny. There is one instinct all dogs share: loyalty to their owners.

"J" is for Jowls,

Dripping with drool.
Pooches who shake them
Could fill up a pool.

Simply put, jowls are droopy cheeks, and they can show up on everyone from humans to pigs. A number of dog breeds have large jowls, including Boxers, Bulldogs, Mastiffs, and Saint Bernards. These dogs tend to drool more than others because their saliva pools inside those hanging flaps. When they shake their heads, watch out! You're in for a serious water show.

"K" is for K9 Officer.

Don't mess with the law,
Or you could end up
In a clever dog's jaws.

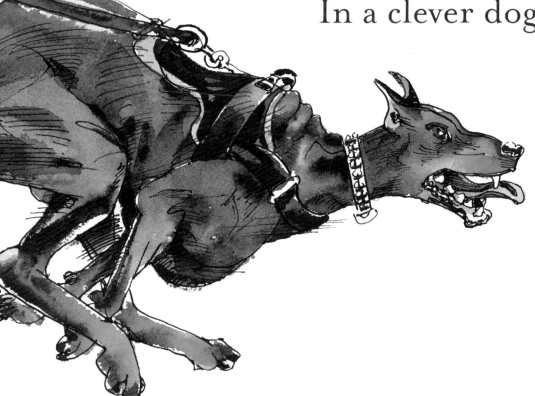

Dogs have assisted law-enforcement officials for **centuries**; records indicate that pooches helped keep the peace in St. Malo, France, as far back as the 14th century. Today, K9 officers sniff for illegal substances, search for missing persons, and chase down bad guys. German Shepherds are among the most common breeds used for this type of work because of their strength and keen sense of smell, but Rottweilers, Doberman Pinschers, and even Beagles have worn badges to protect our communities.

"L" is for Labradors,

Canine overachievers.
They've long been America's
Favorite retrievers.

For 19 years running, Labrador Retrievers have enjoyed the top spot as the most popular dog in America, according to registration statistics compiled by the American Kennel Club. In fact, Providence, Rhode Island, is the only city in the nation in which Labs aren't among the top-five breeds. It's easy to see why Labs are perpetually in demand—they are even-tempered, easy-to-train, and loving toward humans. Originally bred to help fishermen catch fish that escaped from their hooks, Labs' "otter tails" serve as rudders that help them swim against strong currents. These days, their tails are more commonly seen wagging in the breeze as they soak in their parents' love and attention.

"M" is for Mascots,

From Uga to Rhett.

These mighty canines

Ain't cuddly pets.

Good mascots represent strength and tenacity, so it's little wonder that dogs are among the most popular ones in sports. Boston University rallies around a fierce Boston Terrier. BU's colors are scarlet and white, so the terrier's name is Rhett; as anyone who's seen *Gone with the Wind* knows, nobody loves Scarlett more than Rhett. Meanwhile, Uga is the University of Georgia's English Bulldog mascot. He reclines on a bag of ice inside an air-conditioned doghouse when he needs a break during football games. Many other college teams have Bulldog mascots, including Butler, Gonzaga, Mississippi State, Louisiana Tech, and Yale.

"N" is for

Noses

'Cause dogs like to sniff.
You can't cook in peace
Once your hound gets a whiff.

Noses are the portals through which dogs see the **world**. Smelling is their primary sense—they have 220 million receptors in their noses for this purpose, while humans have only 5 million. This makes a dog's sense of smell thousands of times more sensitive than a human's! Is it any wonder, then, that dogs love to hang out in the kitchen when dinner is on the stove? Their sense of smell is also what helps them do amazing things like search for missing persons and detect certain types of cancers in humans.

"O" is for

Obedience,

Keeping Fido on track
And showing him you're the one
Leading the pack.

Of all the virtues a dog can have, obedience is perhaps **the most prized**. Of course, the definition of an obedient dog varies widely—to some, it's a pooch who will come to them in a perfectly straight line during an obedience competition; to others, it's a dog who will simply come. Any dog who competes in a canine sport like disc catching or dock jumping must obey his or her trainer, just like an athlete obeys his or her coach. If you want help teaching your dog obedience, you're in luck: there are a whopping 750 books about the subject on the market.

"P" is for Poodle,

Sheared to perfection.
Their good looks are matched
By their charming affection.

Today, a perfectly coifed poodle is considered fash-
ionable, but hundreds of years ago, it was considered functional. Poodles were actually bred as water retrievers in Germany, and their "Poodle hairdo" allowed them to swim efficiently while still keeping their vital organs and joints warm. Poodles come in three varieties—standard, miniature, and toy—and in a variety of colors. Loving and highly intelligent, they are among the top-10 most popular dogs in the country, according to the American Kennel Club.

"Q" is for

Quarters—

Dogs must have their own:
Sometimes a couch
Is as good as a throne.

Most pooches have a place inside their homes that **they think belongs only to them**. That place may be a velvet dog bed with a built-in neck pillow, an electric warmer, and their name monogrammed on the front. Or it may simply be the coziest side of the family couch. For certain small breeds, a tight spot beneath the bed is where they feel safest from danger. But regardless of what their quarters looks like, most dogs have a "happy place" that appeals to their natural instincts as den animals.

"R" is for

Runts—

The ones who start small
Are often the biggest
Treasures of all.

Every litter of puppies has its runt—the one who's smaller and weaker than the rest. But don't feel too sorry for this tiny pooch; as he learns how to jockey for milk without getting trampled, he just might become the smartest and most dominant one of all. And like Clifford the Big Red Dog (literature's most famous runt), the teensiest of puppies could grow up to be largest of adult dogs—and the sweetest.

"S" is for Shih Tzus,

They care and they show it.
But if you displease them,
They'll bark 'til you know it.

Bred in China more than 1,000 years ago, Shih Tzus are a pampered breed who served as house pets for most of the Ming Dynasty. Their name means "lion," and it's easy to see why—their long, luxurious coat resembles a lion's mane, and they certainly consider themselves kings of their own jungles! As anyone who has crossed this breed knows, they aren't scared to bark when they're upset, but they're also prized for their playfulness and loving temperament. For more than five years running, Shih Tzus have ranked among the top-10 breeds in the country, according to the American Kennel Club.

"T" is for Toto.

Movie buffs old and new
Have fallen for Dorothy
And her little dog, too.

When *The Wizard of Oz* **was released on the big screen in 1939**, it featured Judy Garland as Dorothy Gale and a black Cairn Terrier named Terry as Dorothy's sidekick, Toto. Terry was actually a female who was paid a salary of $125 per week; some of the movie's human actors received a third of that. But Terry had the acting chops to command top dollar for her work—she had actually appeared in more than a dozen films, sharing the screen with everyone from Shirley Temple to Spencer Tracy. In 2001, movie producer Willard Carroll wrote a book about Terry's life called *I Toto*.

"U" is for

Unconditional;

Your dog will always be there

If a jerk steals your job

Or a punk cuts your hair.

If there's one thing we can learn from dogs, it's how to love well. Dogs don't pay attention to outward appearances, and they don't care how much money their parents make. They never hold grudges, and they always seem to give their best greetings after their loved ones have had a bad day. Dogs, it is said, are man's best friend—and in homes across the world, they prove it time and time again.

"V" is for Vets.

Dogs like them a lot—
Unless, of course,
It's time for a shot.

There are more than 60,000 veterinarians in the **United States**, and the majority of them work with dogs. They vaccinate, medicate, and placate our pups—and no pooch or his parent could get along without them. As the number of households with dogs grows, so too will the number of veterinarians; the Bureau of Labor Statistics predicts that the field will expand as much as 35 percent over the next decade. It also expects that the number of veterinarians with specific areas of expertise, like food science or oncology, will grow.

"W" is for

Wag.

Thrilled or subdued,
A dog's tail will tell you
Exactly his mood.

Dog tails may be long or short, curved or straight, **furry or smooth**. But all tails help humans interpret how a dog is feeling. A relaxed pooch will hold his tail in a natural position, while a submissive dog may tuck it between her legs. A cheerful dog may wag his tail wildly, and another might even move hers in circles to show her enthusiasm. Still, not all wags mean good things—some dogs wiggle their tails when they feel threatened, signaling they're willing to attack. And still others hold their tails stiff, or "flag" them, when they're on high alert. So lest we wag the dog, we should note that a dog's entire body helps translate the meaning of his or her tail—not the other way around.

"X" marks the spot
Where dogs bury their bones.
How they can find them
Is one of life's great unknowns.

How is it that we can't find a set of keys we had in our hands an hour ago, but dogs can find bones they buried last winter? And what is it about certain bushes or fire hydrants that makes a pooch want to lift his leg and relieve himself, no matter how many times we've begged him to stop? Whether for hoarding or for marking, dogs have certain spots they return to over and over—it's one of the wonders (and frustrations!) of canine intelligence. Now if only they could sniff out the spot where we left our keys...

"Y" is for

Yorkies—

Small but courageous.

Their bold confidence

Is often contagious.

The biggest of Yorkshire Terriers weighs less than seven pounds, but don't tell this breed they're small—they're known for their bravery and have no problem sticking up for themselves. Yorkies got their name from Yorkshire, the English region in which they were bred during the 19th century. They were originally intended to hunt rats in clothing mills, but their tenacity and adorable looks wowed wealthy Europeans, many of whom took them in as pampered pets. Yorkies have jumped in popularity among Americans in recent years—in 1999 they were the ninth most-registered breed, and in 2009 they were the third most-registered breed.

"Z" is for

ZZZs–

Pooches love to saw logs.

In our next lives

We should come back as dogs.

The average dog snoozes 14 hours a day, which means he spends more than half his life getting some shut-eye. Working dogs, like those who herd cattle on ranches, tend to sleep less, while purely domestic dogs may sleep even more. Research has shown that dogs can enter deep rapid-eye-movement (REM) sleep during their naps, which means it is likely that dogs have dreams—this explains your pooch's occasional twitching, whining, and eye fluttering while he's snoozing. Several breeds tend to snore, including Pekinese, Pugs, and Boston Terriers, and overweight dogs or dogs with allergies may rock the house, too. Cover your ears—they'll probably be sleeping another few hours.

Order an 18" x 24" poster of your favorite dog at:

This book is available in quantity at special discounts for your group or organization. For further information, contact:

Triumph Books
542 South Dearborn Street
Suite 750
Chicago, Illinois 60605
312. 939. 3330
Fax 312. 663. 3557
www.triumphbooks.com

Printed in China
ISBN 978–1–60078–371–5